STARS
UNLIMITED™

Designs by Dereck Lockwood

HOUSE of
WHITE
BIRCHES
PUBLISHERS
SINCE 1947

2

Table of Contents

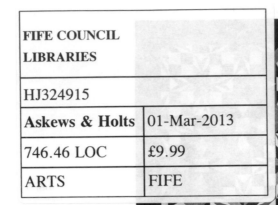

Star Flower,
page 38

Starscape,
page 10

Galaxia,
page 26

Aubrielle

Project Notes

Most border stripes contain both narrow and wide stripes that repeat across the fabric width. The fabric used for this project has a wide stripe bordered by a narrow stripe. Because of the width of the strips and the ¼" seam allowance, you can only get two repeat strips from the fabric. The finished width of the border stripe used in this quilt is 11". Your border width could vary, which will change the size of the finished quilt. Refer to instructions for making Y seams on page 47 wherever Y seams are referenced in these instructions.

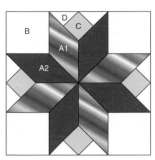

Aubrielle Star
11" x 11" Block
Make 17

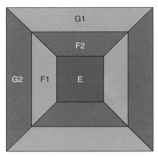

Window
11" x 11" Block
Make 32

Project Specifications

Skill Level: Advanced
Quilt Size: 99" x 99"
Block Size: 11" x 11"
Number of Blocks: 49

Materials

- ⅜ yard gold tonal
- ⅝ yard black print
- ¾ yard rust mottled
- 1½ yards cream rose print
- 2¼ yards dark green print
- 3 yards light green print
- 6 yards border stripe with black background
- Batting 107" x 107"
- Backing 107" x 107"
- All-purpose thread to match fabrics
- Quilting thread
- Template material
- Water-soluble blue pen
- Basic sewing tools and supplies

Cutting

1. Lay out the 6-yard length of border stripe. Select the first border stripe (one wide stripe motif bordered by two narrow stripe motifs), add ¼" to each side of the motif and cut a strip along the full length of the fabric. Repeat to cut a second strip. *Note: Excess fabric will be used to cut A1 pieces.*

2. Cut each of the strips cut in step 1 in half to make four identical H strips for mitered-corner borders.

3. Prepare templates using patterns given; cut as directed on each piece, using the leftover border fabric to cut the A1 pieces. Transfer seam dots (shown as red dots on patterns) to each piece as marked on patterns.

4. Cut (10) 2¼" by fabric width strips light green print for binding.

Completing the Aubrielle Star Blocks

1. Select four each A1, A2, B and C pieces and eight D pieces for one block.

2. Sew an A1 piece to an A2 piece to make an A unit, stitching from dot to dot as shown in Figure 1; press seam open. Repeat to make four A units.

Figure 1

3. Set B into an A unit using a Y seam, starting stitching on one side at the inside dot on A and stitching all the way to the outside edge as shown in Figure 2; repeat with second seam. Press seams toward the A unit, again referring to Figure 2. Repeat with the remaining three B squares and A units.

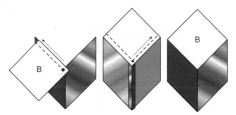

Figure 2

4. Join two A-B units as shown in Figure 3; press seams open. Repeat to make a second A-B unit.

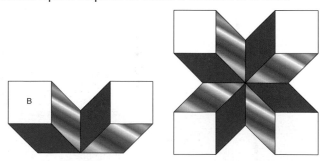

Figure 3   **Figure 4**

5. Join the two A-B units to complete an open block as shown in Figure 4; press seams open.

6. Sew D to two adjacent sides of C to make a C-D unit as shown in Figure 5, making sure that seam dot on C is at outer point; press seams toward D. Repeat to make a total of four C-D units.

Figure 5

7. Starting at the inside marked dots on the A pieces, and stitching to the outside edge using a Y seam, set a C-D unit into each opening in the open block as shown in Figure 6; press seams toward the A pieces.

Figure 6

8. Repeat steps 1–7 to complete a total of 17 Aubrielle Star blocks.

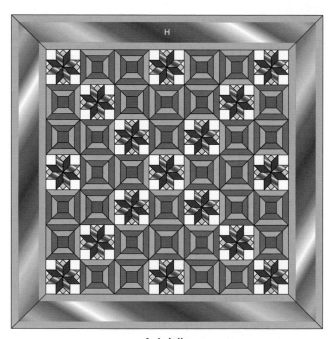

Aubrielle
Placement Diagram 99" x 99"

Completing the Window Blocks

1. To complete one Window block, sew an F1 piece to a G2 piece to make an F1-G2 unit as shown in Figure 7; press seam toward G2. Repeat to make a second F1-G2 unit.

Figure 7

2. Repeat step 1 with one each F2 and G1 piece to make a F2-G1 unit, as shown in Figure 8; press seam toward G1. Repeat to make a second F2-G1 unit.

Figure 8

3. Sew an F1-G2 unit to opposite sides of an E square using a Y seam, starting and stopping stitching at the dots as shown in Figure 9; press seams open.

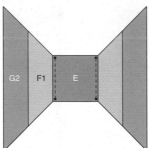

Figure 9

4. Sew an F2-G1 unit to the remaining sides of the pieced unit as in step 3, beginning stitching at the E dot and sewing from E to the outside edges on each side to complete the block as shown in Figure 10; press seams open.

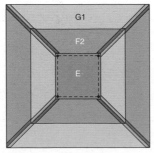

Figure 10

5. Repeat steps 1–4 to complete a total of 32 Window blocks.

Completing the Quilt Top

1. Join three Aubrielle Star blocks with four Window blocks to make an X row as shown in Figure 11; press seams to one side. Repeat to make three X rows.

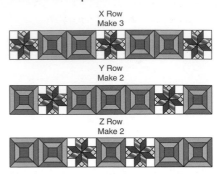

Figure 11

2. Join two Aubrielle Star blocks with five Window blocks to make a Y row, again referring to Figure 11; press seams to one side. Repeat to make two Y rows.

3. Join two Aubrielle Star blocks with five Window blocks to make a Z row, again referring to Figure 11; press seams to one side. Repeat to make two Z rows.

4. Join the X, Y and Z rows referring to Figure 12, turning rows so seams in adjoining rows face in opposite directions as shown in Figure 13; press seams in one direction.

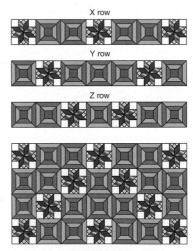

Figure 12

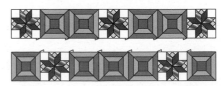

Figure 13

5. Fold the quilt top in half horizontally and vertically and crease to mark the centers. Fold each H strip in half and crease to mark the centers.

6. Center and sew an H strip to each side of the pieced center, stopping stitching ¼" from each end of the quilt top as shown in Figure 14.

Figure 14

7. Join the H strips at each corner at a 45-degree angle, matching stripes as shown in Figure 15.

Figure 15

8. Trim seam allowance to ¼" and press mitered seams open and long seams toward H strips.

9. The quilt top is ready for quilting and binding as desired. See page 47 for finishing instructions. ❖

The back of the quilt shows off the beautiful quilting.

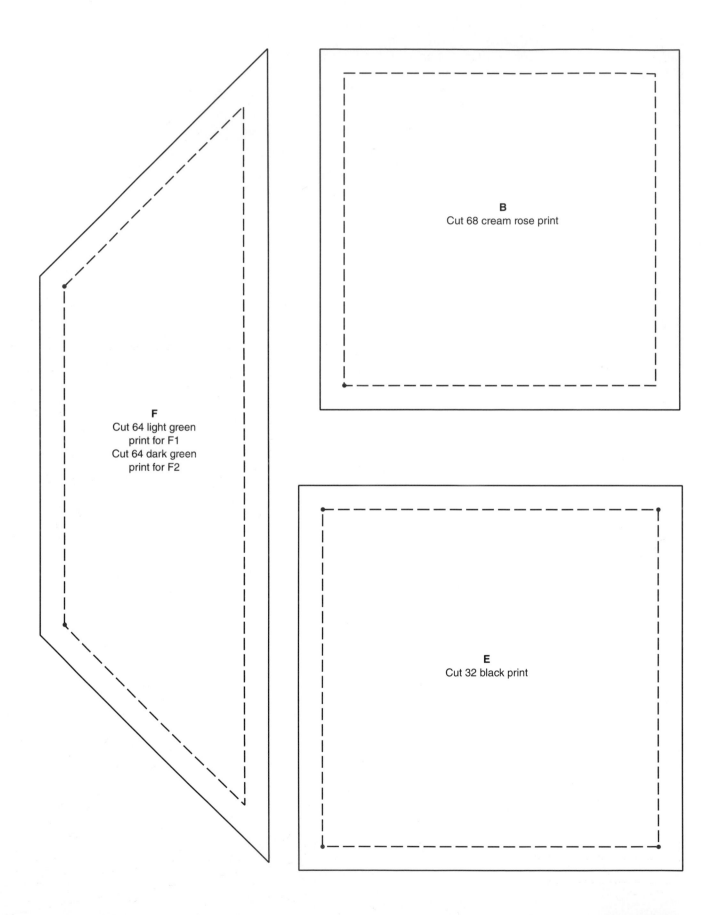

F
Cut 64 light green
print for F1
Cut 64 dark green
print for F2

B
Cut 68 cream rose print

E
Cut 32 black print

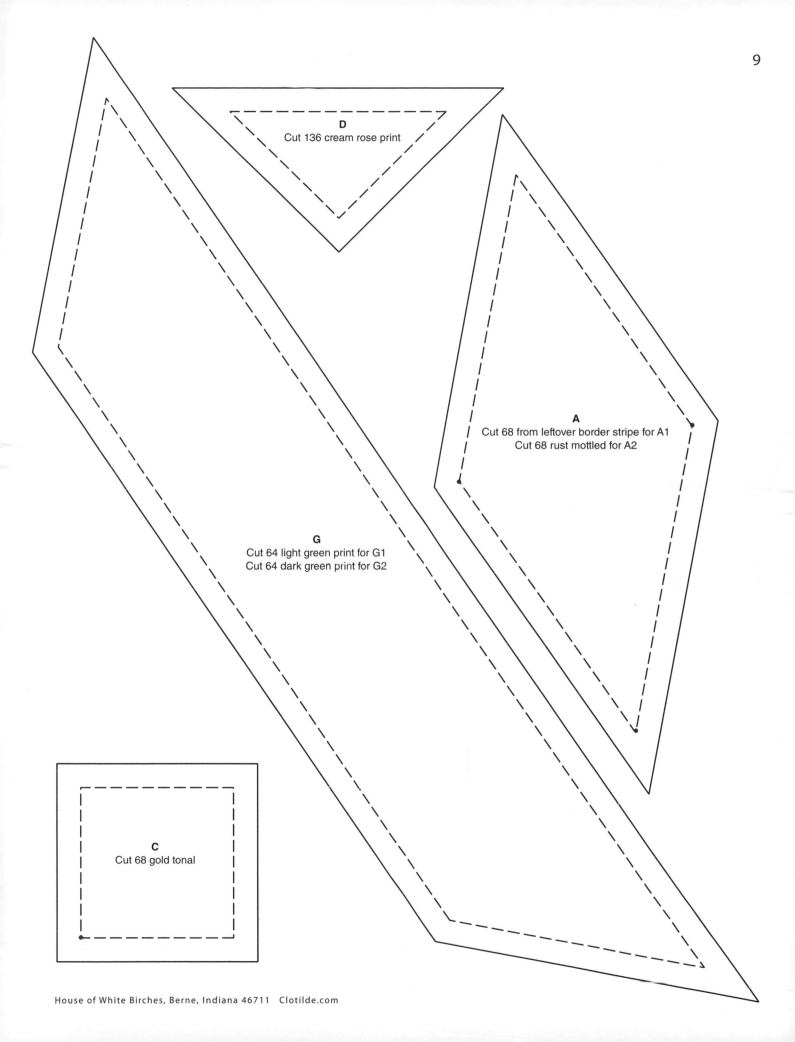

D
Cut 136 cream rose print

A
Cut 68 from leftover border stripe for A1
Cut 68 rust mottled for A2

G
Cut 64 light green print for G1
Cut 64 dark green print for G2

C
Cut 68 gold tonal

Starscape

Project Specifications
Skill Level: Advanced
Quilt Size: 92" x 92"
Block Size: 9" x 9"
Number of Blocks: 61

Materials
- ⅜ yard gold mottled
- 1¼ yards red roses tonal
- 1½ yards dark green polka dot
- 1⅓ yards light green mottled
- 2½ yards red leaf print
- 5¼ yards cream floral tonal
- Batting 100" x 100"
- Backing 100" x 100"
- All-purpose thread to match fabrics
- Quilting thread
- Template material
- Water-soluble blue pen
- Basic sewing tools and supplies

Cutting
1. Prepare templates using patterns given; cut as directed on each piece.

2. Cut two 14" by fabric width strips cream floral tonal; subcut strips into (5) 14" squares. Cut each square on both diagonals to make 20 K triangles.

3. Cut one 7¼" by fabric width strips cream floral tonal; subcut strip into two 7¼" squares. Cut each square in half on one diagonal to make four L triangles.

4. Cut eight 2¼" by fabric width strips dark green polka dot. Join strips on the short ends to make one long strip; press seams open. Subcut strip into two 77" M strips and two 80½" N strips. *Note: Measure all sides of your pieced center before cutting strips to length to be sure of the finished size of your quilt center. All sides should measure the same. The sizes given are the correct mathematical sizes if all stitching is perfect.*

5. Cut nine 6½" by fabric width strips red leaf print. Join strips on the short ends to make one long strip; press seams open. Subcut strip into two 80½" O strips and two 92½" P strips.

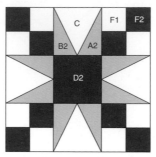

Garden Star
9" x 9" Block
Make 4

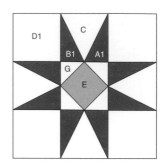

Star Rays
9" x 9" Block
Make 9

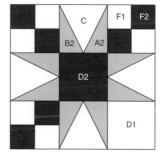

Garden Star Variation
9" x 9" Block
Make 12

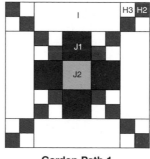

Garden Path 1
9" x 9" Block
Make 20

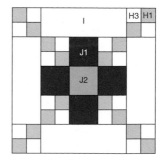

Garden Path 2
9" x 9" Block
Make 16

6. Cut (10) 2¼" by fabric width strips red leaf print for binding.

Completing the Star Rays Blocks
1. Select one gold E square, four cream G triangles, four each dark green A1 and B1 triangles, four cream C triangles and four cream D1 squares for one block.

2. To complete one block, sew G to each side of E to make a center unit as shown in Figure 1; press seams toward E.

Figure 1   **Figure 2**

3. Sew A1 and B1 to C as shown in Figure 2 to make a side unit; press seams away from C. Repeat to make four side units.

Tip

It is important that the A1 and B1 pieces are sewn together with C perfectly to achieve a 3½" x 3½" square when the unit is finished. Transfer the alignment markings on the patterns to the fabric pieces using a water-soluble blue pen. Use these marks for matching the edges of the pieces before sewing as shown in Figure 3 to make perfect units every time!

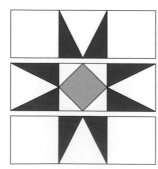

Figure 3

4. Sew a side unit to opposite sides of the center unit to make the center row as shown in Figure 4; press seams toward the center unit.

Figure 4   **Figure 5**

5. Sew a D1 square to opposite sides of a side unit to make a row as shown in Figure 5; press seams toward D1. Repeat to make a second row.

6. Sew a row made in step 5 to opposite sides of the center row to complete one Star Rays block referring to Figure 6; press seams away from the center row.

7. Repeat steps 1–6 to complete a total of nine Star Rays blocks.

Figure 6

Completing the Garden Star Blocks

1. Select one red D2 square, four each light green A2 and B2 triangles, four cream C triangles and eight each cream F1 and red F2 squares for one block.

2. To complete one block, sew A2 and B2 to C as shown in Figure 7 to make a side unit; press seams away from C. Repeat to make four side units.

Figure 7   **Figure 8**

3. Sew F1 to F2 to make an F unit as shown in Figure 8; press seam toward F2. Repeat to make eight F units.

4. Join two F units to make a corner unit as shown in Figure 9; press seam to one side. Repeat to make four corner units.

Figure 9   **Figure 10**

5. Sew a side unit to opposite sides of the D2 square to complete the center row as shown in Figure 10; press seams toward center unit.

6. Sew a corner unit to opposite sides of a side unit to make a row as shown in Figure 11; press seams toward corner units. Repeat to make a second row.

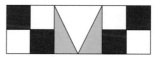

Figure 11

7. Sew a row made in step 6 to opposite sides of the center row to complete one Garden Star block referring to Figure 12; press seams away from the center row.

Figure 12

8. Repeat steps 1–7 to complete a total of four Garden Star blocks.

Completing the Garden Star Variation Blocks

1. Select one red D2 square, four each light green A2 and B2 triangles, four cream C triangles, one cream D1 and six each cream F1 and red F2 squares for one block.

2. Repeat steps 2–4 for Completing the Garden Star Blocks except make only six F units and combine to make three corner units.

3. Sew a side unit to opposite sides of D2 to complete the center row, again referring to Figure 10; press seams toward D2.

4. Sew a corner unit to opposite sides of a side unit to make the top row, again referring to Figure 11; press seams toward corner units.

5. Sew a corner unit to one side and a D1 square to the opposite side of the remaining side unit to complete the bottom row as shown in Figure 13; press seams away from side unit.

Figure 13

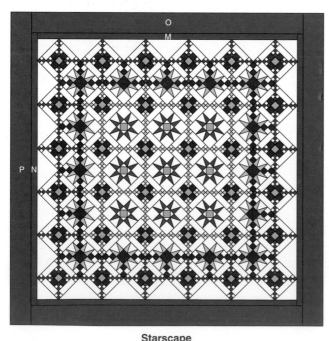

Starscape
Placement Diagram 92" x 92"

6. Sew the top row made in step 4 to the top of the center row and the bottom row made in step 5 to the bottom of the center row as shown in Figure 14 to complete one Garden Star Variation block; press seams away from the center row.

Figure 14

7. Repeat steps 1–6 to complete a total of 12 Garden Star Variation blocks.

Completing the Garden Path 1 Blocks

1. Select one gold J2 and four red J1 squares, 16 each dark green H2 and cream H3 squares, and four I rectangles for one block.

2. Sew an H2 square to an H3 square; press seam toward H2. Repeat to make 16 units. Join two units to make an H unit as shown in Figure 15; press seam to one side. Repeat to make a total of eight H units.

Figure 15

3. Sew a J1 square to opposite sides of the J2 square to make a J2 row; press seams toward J1.

4. Sew an H unit to opposite sides of a J1 square to make a J1 row as shown in Figure 16; press seam toward J1. Repeat to make a second J1 row.

Figure 16

5. Sew a J1 row to opposite sides of the J2 row to complete the block center as shown in Figure 17; press seams toward the J2 row.

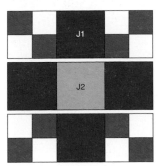

Figure 17

6. Sew an I rectangle to opposite sides of the block center; press seams toward I.

7. Sew an H unit to opposite ends of each of the remaining I rectangles as shown in Figure 18; press seams toward I.

Figure 18

8. Sew these units to the remaining sides of the center unit to complete one Garden Path 1 block referring to Figure 19; press seams away from the block center.

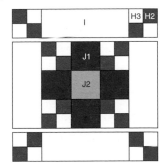

Figure 19

9. Repeat steps 1–8 to complete a total of 20 Garden Path 1 blocks.

Completing the Garden Path 2 Blocks

1. Refer to steps 1–8 for Completing the Garden Path 1 blocks, substituting light green H1 squares for the H2 dark green squares to make a total of 16 blocks referring to Figure 20.

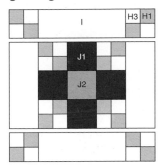

Figure 20

Completing the Quilt Top

1. Arrange and join the blocks in rows with the K and L triangles referring to Figure 21.

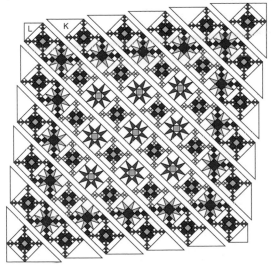

Figure 21

2. Join the rows referring to the Placement Diagram and Figure 21 for positioning to complete the quilt center; press seams in one direction.

3. Sew the M strips to the top and bottom, and N strips to opposite sides of the quilt center; press seams toward M and N strips.

4. Sew the O strips to the top and bottom, and the P strips to opposite sides of the pieced center to complete the quilt top.

5. The quilt top is ready for quilting and binding as desired. See page 47 for finishing instructions. ❖

The back of the quilt shows off the beautiful quilting.

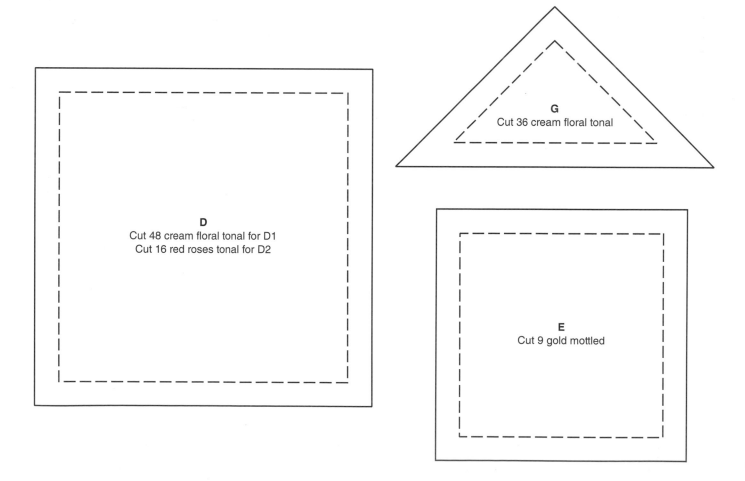

D
Cut 48 cream floral tonal for D1
Cut 16 red roses tonal for D2

G
Cut 36 cream floral tonal

E
Cut 9 gold mottled

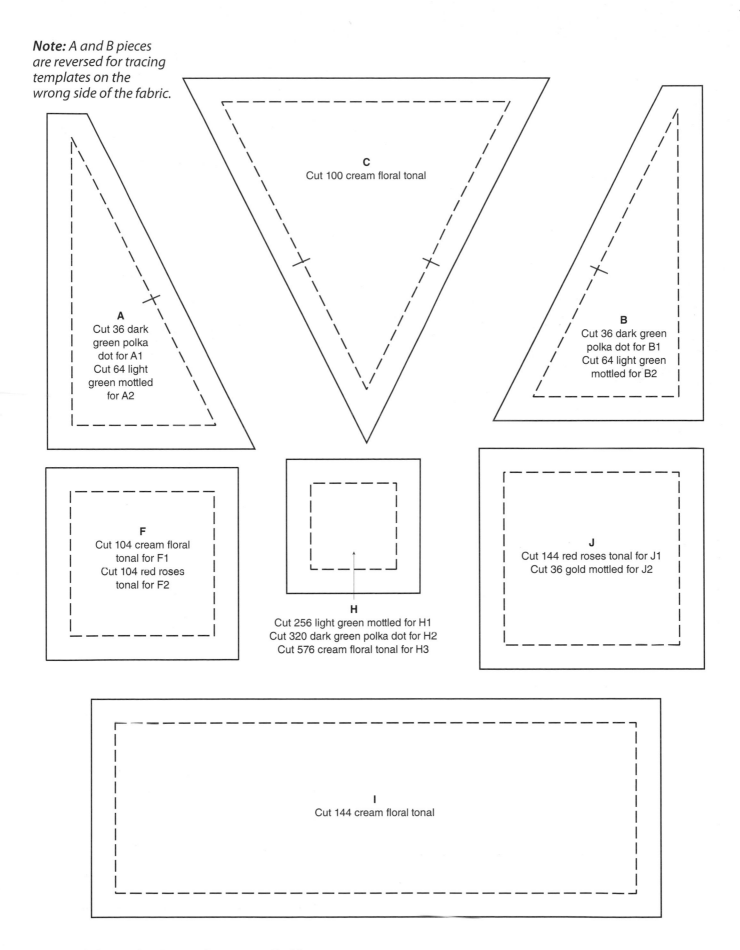

Note: *A and B pieces are reversed for tracing templates on the wrong side of the fabric.*

C
Cut 100 cream floral tonal

A
Cut 36 dark green polka dot for A1
Cut 64 light green mottled for A2

B
Cut 36 dark green polka dot for B1
Cut 64 light green mottled for B2

F
Cut 104 cream floral tonal for F1
Cut 104 red roses tonal for F2

H
Cut 256 light green mottled for H1
Cut 320 dark green polka dot for H2
Cut 576 cream floral tonal for H3

J
Cut 144 red roses tonal for J1
Cut 36 gold mottled for J2

I
Cut 144 cream floral tonal

Lavender Lace

Project Specifications
Skill Level: Advanced
Quilt Size: 83" x 107"
Block Size: 12" x 12"
Number of Blocks: 35

Materials
- 1 yard light gold mottled
- 1⅜ yards lavender mottled
- 2⅛ yards purple rose tonal
- 2¾ yards cream tonal
- 3¼ yards green print
- Batting 91" x 115"
- Backing 91" x 115"
- All-purpose thread to match fabrics
- Quilting thread
- Template material
- Water-soluble blue pen
- Basic sewing tools and supplies

Cutting
1. Prepare templates using patterns given; cut as directed on each piece.

2. Cut (17) 2½" by fabric width strips green print. Join strips on short ends to make one long strip; press seams open. Subcut strip into two each 84½" I, 64½" J, 103½" M and 83½" N strips.

3. Cut (10) 2¼" by fabric width strips green print for binding.

4. Cut nine 8" by fabric width strips purple rose tonal. Join strips on short ends to make one long strip; press seams open. Subcut strip into two 88½" K strips and two 79½" L strips.

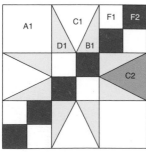

Block 1
12" x 12" Block
Make 6

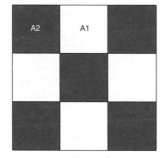

Block 2
12" x 12" Block
Make 4

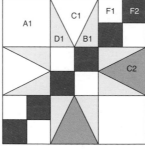

Block 3
12" x 12" Block
Make 11

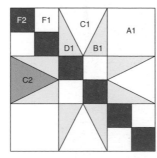

Block 4
12" x 12" Block
Make 4

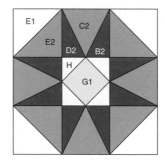

Block 5
12" x 12" Block
Make 4

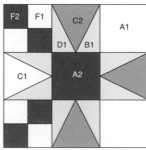

Block 6
12" x 12" Block
Make 2

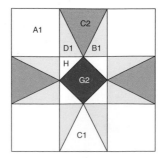

Block 7
12" x 12" Block
Make 4

Completing the Pieced Units

1. Sew an H triangle to each side of a G1 square to complete a G1-H unit as shown in Figure 1; press seams toward H. Repeat to make a total of 11 G1-H units.

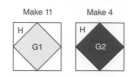

Make 11   Make 4

Figure 1

2. Sew an H triangle to each side of a G2 square to complete a G2-H unit, again referring to Figure 1; press seams toward H. Repeat to make a total of four G2-H units.

3. Sew an F1 square to an F2 square to make an F1-F2 unit; press seam toward F2. Repeat to make 80 F1-F2 units.

4. Select two F1-F2 units and join as shown in Figure 2 to complete an F unit; press seam to one side. Repeat to make a total of 40 F units.

Make 40

Figure 2

5. Sew B1 to one side and D1 to the opposite side of C1 to make a C1 unit as shown in Figure 3; press seams away from C1. Repeat to make a total of 38 C1 units.

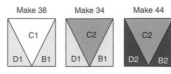

Make 38   Make 34   Make 44

Figure 3

6. Sew B1 to one side and D1 to the opposite side of C2 to make a C2 unit, again referring to Figure 3; press seams away from C2. Repeat to make a total of 34 C2 units.

7. Sew B2 to one side and D2 to the opposite side of C2 to complete C2-B2-D2 unit, again referring to Figure 3; press seams away from C2. Repeat to make a total of 44 C2-B2-D2 units.

8. Sew E1 to E2 to make an E unit as shown in Figure 4; press seam toward E2. Repeat to make a total of 44 E units.

Make 44

9. Sew an A2 square between two A1 squares to make an A1 unit referring to Figure 5; press seams toward A2. Repeat to make a total of six A1 units.

Figure 4

Make 6   Make 12

Figure 5

10. Sew an A1 square between two A2 squares to make an A2 unit as shown in Figure 5; press seams toward A2. Repeat to make a total of 12 A2 units.

Completing Block 1

1. Sew an A1 row between two A2 rows to complete Block 1 as shown in Figure 6; press seams to one side.

Make 6

Figure 6

Lavender Lace
Placement Diagram 83" x 107"

2. Repeat step 1 to make a total of six Block 1 blocks.

Completing Block 2

1. Sew A1 to one side and an F unit to the opposite side of a C1 unit to make a row as shown in Figure 7; press seams away from the C1 unit.

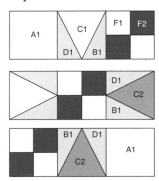

2. Sew a C1 unit to one side and a C2 unit to the opposite side of an F unit to make a row, again referring to Figure 7; press seams toward the F unit.

Figure 7

3. Sew an F unit to one side and A1 to the opposite side of a C2 unit to make a row, again referring to Figure 7; press seams away from the C2 unit.

4. Join the rows as stitched referring to Figure 8 to complete one Block 2 block; press seams away from the center row.

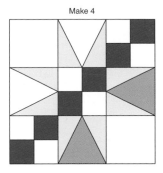

Figure 8

5. Repeat steps 1–4 to complete a total of four Block 2 blocks.

Completing Block 3

1. Sew an E unit to opposite sides of a C2-B2-D2 unit to make a row as shown in Figure 9; press seams toward E units. Repeat to make a second row.

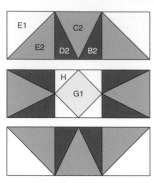

Figure 9

2. Sew a C2-B2-D2 unit to opposite sides of a G1-H unit to make a row, again referring to Figure 9; press seam toward the G1-H unit.

3. Join the rows referring to Figure 10 to complete one Block 3 block; press seams away from the center row.

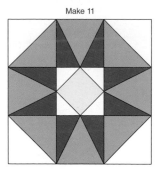

Make 11

Figure 10

4. Repeat steps 1–3 to complete a total of 11 Block 3 blocks.

Completing Block 4

1. Sew A1 to one side and an F unit to the opposite side of a C1 unit to make a row as shown in Figure 11; press seams toward the C1 unit. Repeat to make a second row.

2. Sew a C1 unit to one side and a C2 unit to opposite sides of an F unit to make a row, again referring to Figure 11.

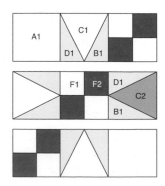

Figure 11

3. Join the rows to complete one Block 4 block referring to Figure 12; press seams toward center row.

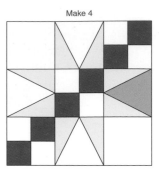

Make 4

Figure 12

4. Repeat steps 1–3 to complete a total of four Block 4 blocks.

Completing Block 5

1. Sew an F unit to one side and A1 to the opposite side of a C1 unit to make a row as shown in Figure 13; press seams away from the C1 unit. Repeat to make a second row.

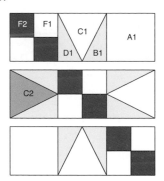

Figure 13

2. Sew a C1 unit to one side and a C2 unit to opposite sides of an F unit to make a row, again referring to Figure 13; press seams toward the F unit.

3. Join the rows referring to Figure 14 to complete one Block 5 block; press seams toward the center row.

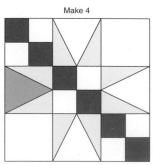

Make 4

Figure 14

4. Repeat steps 1–3 to complete a total of four Block 5 blocks.

Completing Block 6

1. Sew an F unit to one side and A1 to the opposite side of a C2 unit to make a row as shown in Figure 15; press seams away from the F unit.

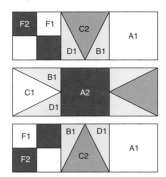

Figure 15

2. Sew a C1 unit to one side and a C2 unit to the opposite sides of an A2 square to make a row, again referring to Figure 15; press seams toward A2.

3. Sew an F unit to one side and an A1 unit to the opposite side of a C2 unit to make a row, again referring to Figure 15; press seams away from the C2 unit. *Note: This row is the same as the row pieced in step 1 except that the C2 unit is turned.*

4. Join the rows referring to Figure 16 to complete one Block 6 block; press seams toward the center row.

Make 2

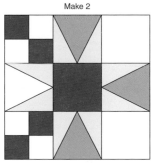

Figure 16

5. Repeat steps 1–4 to make a second Block 6 block.

Completing Block 7

1. Sew an A1 square to opposite sides of a C2 unit to complete a row as shown in Figure 17; press seams toward A1 squares.

2. Sew a C2 unit to opposite sides of a G2-H unit to complete a row, again referring to Figure 17; press seams toward the G2-H unit.

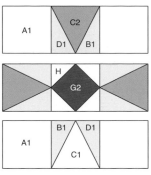

Figure 17

3. Sew an A1 square to opposite sides of a C1 unit to make a row, again referring to Figure 17; press seams toward A1 squares.

4. Join the rows as shown in Figure 18 to complete one Block 7 block; press seams toward the center row.

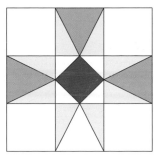

Figure 18

5. Repeat steps 1–4 to complete a total of four Block 7 blocks.

Completing the Quilt Top

1. To make Row 1, join blocks in this order: 1, 2, 3, 2 and 1, turning blocks as necessary referring to Figure 19 on page 24; press seams toward the left.

2. To make Row 2, join blocks in this order: 4, 3, 7, 3 and 5, turning blocks as necessary referring to Figure 19 on page 24; press seams to the right.

3. To make Row 3, join blocks in this order: 5, 3, 7, 3 and 4, turning blocks as necessary referring to Figure 19 on page 24; press seams toward the left.

4. To make Row 4, join blocks in this order: 1, 6, 3, 6 and 1, turning blocks as necessary referring to Figure 19 on page 24; press seams to the right.

5. To make Row 5, join blocks in this order: 4, 3, 7, 3 and 5, turning blocks as necessary referring to Figure 19 on page 24; press seams toward the left.

6. To make Row 6, join blocks in this order: 5, 3, 7, 3 and 4, turning blocks as necessary referring to Figure 19; press seams to the right.

7. To make Row 7, join blocks in this order: 1, 2, 3, 2 and 1, turning blocks as necessary referring to Figure 19; press seams toward the left.

8. Join the rows in numerical order to complete the pieced center; press seams in one direction.

9. Sew an I strip to opposite long sides and J strips to the top and bottom of the pieced center; press seams toward I and J strips.

10. Sew a K strip to opposite long sides and L strips to the top and bottom of the pieced center; press seams toward K and L strips.

11. Sew an M strip to opposite long sides and N strips to the top and bottom of the pieced center; press seams toward M and N strips to complete the quilt top.

12. The quilt top is ready for quilting and binding as desired. See page 47 for finishing instructions. ❖

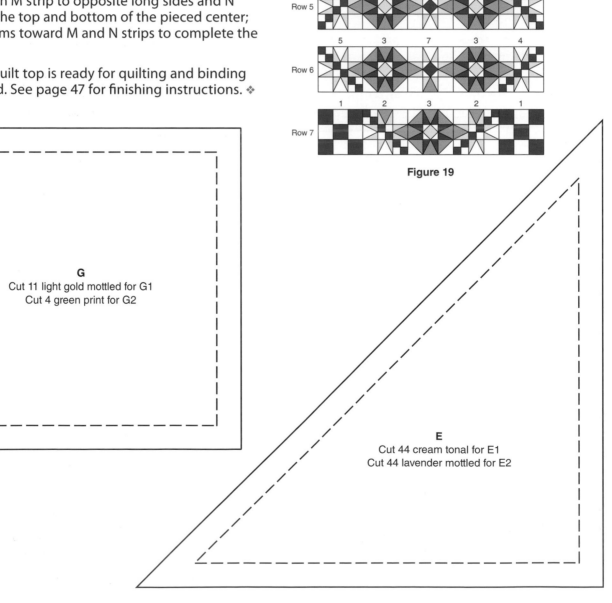

Figure 19

G
Cut 11 light gold mottled for G1
Cut 4 green print for G2

E
Cut 44 cream tonal for E1
Cut 44 lavender mottled for E2

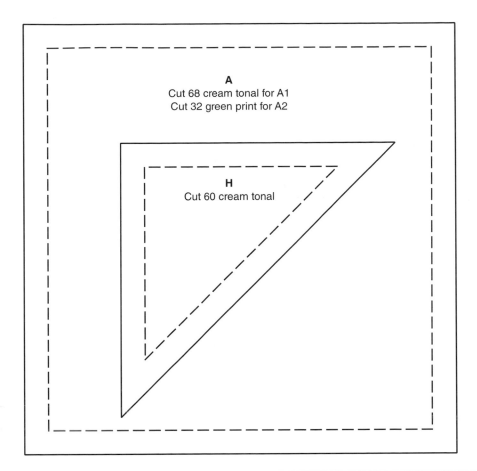

A
Cut 68 cream tonal for A1
Cut 32 green print for A2

H
Cut 60 cream tonal

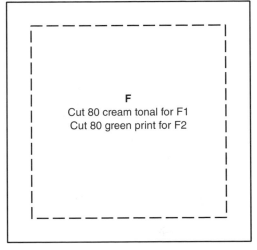

F
Cut 80 cream tonal for F1
Cut 80 green print for F2

Note: B and D pieces are reversed for tracing templates on the wrong side of the fabric.

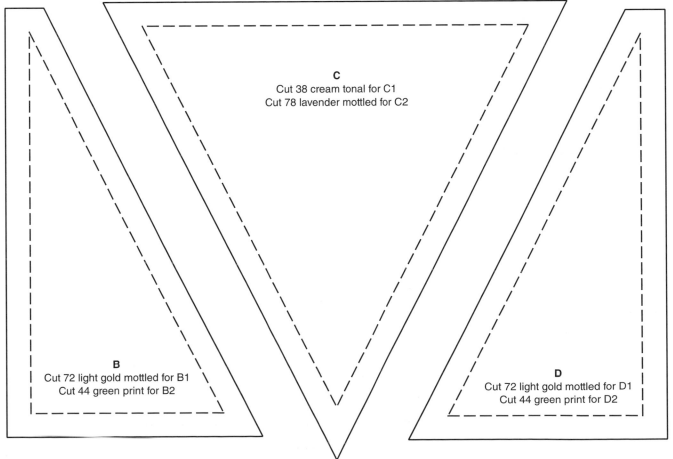

C
Cut 38 cream tonal for C1
Cut 78 lavender mottled for C2

B
Cut 72 light gold mottled for B1
Cut 44 green print for B2

D
Cut 72 light gold mottled for D1
Cut 44 green print for D2

House of White Birches, Berne, Indiana 46711 Clotilde.com

Galaxia

Project Note
Refer to instructions for making Y seams on page 47 wherever Y seams are referenced in these instructions.

Project Specifications
Skill Level: Advanced
Quilt Size: 71½" x 71½"
Block Sizes: 3⁹⁄₁₆" x 3⁹⁄₁₆", 7⅛" x 7⅛", 7½" x 7½"
and 14¼" x 14¼"
Number of Blocks: 20, 28, 32 and 1

Materials
- ¾ yard light violet mottled
- ¾ yard deep violet mottled
- ⅞ yard light gold tonal
- 1 yard gold tonal
- 1⅜ yards light green print
- 2¾ yards cream rose print
- 3¼ yards dark green print
- Batting 84" x 84"
- Backing 84" x 84"
- All-purpose thread to match fabrics
- Quilting thread
- Template material
- Water-soluble blue pen
- Basic sewing tools and supplies

Cutting
1. Prepare templates using patterns given; cut as directed on each piece. Transfer seam dots (shown as red dots on patterns) to each piece as marked on patterns. *Note: To cut a mirror-imaged pair, fold the fabric so it is right sides together; mark around the template and cut out two pieces at once.*

2. Cut eight 6¼" x 6¼" squares cream rose print. Cut each square on both diagonals to make 32 DD triangles.

3. Cut two 6" x 6" squares cream rose print. Cut each square in half on one diagonal to make four EE triangles.

4. Cut four 1¹¹⁄₁₆" x 29" strips each gold tonal (AA), light violet (BB) and deep violet (CC).

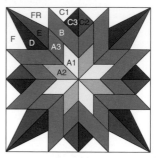

Center Star
14¼" x 14¼" Block
Make 1

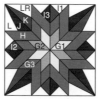

Outer Star
7⅛" x 7⅛" Block
Make 12

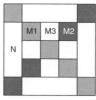

Center Nine-Patch
7⅛" x 7⅛" Block
Make 12

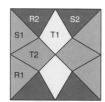

Large Gold Star
7⅛" x 7⅛" Block
Make 4

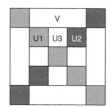

Border Nine-Patch
7½" x 7½" Block
Make 28

Corner Star
7½" x 7½" Block
Make 4

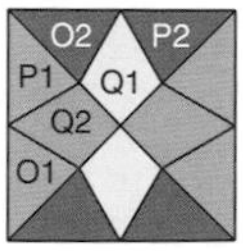

Small Gold Star
3⁹⁄₁₆" x 3⁹⁄₁₆" Block
Make 20

5. Cut five 1½" by fabric width strips dark green print. Join strips on short ends to make one long strip; press seams open. Subcut strip into two 51⅛" FF strips and two 53⅛" GG strips.

6. Cut eight 2½" by fabric width strips dark green print. Join strips on short ends to make one long strip; press seams open. Subcut strip into two 68" HH strips and two 72" II strips.

7. Cut eight 2¼" by fabric width strips dark green print for binding.

Completing the Center Star Block

1. To complete the Center Star block, select four each A1, A2, C2, C3, D, E, F and FR pieces; and eight each A3, B and C1 pieces.

2. Sew an A3 piece to an A2 piece as shown in Figure 1; press seam toward A3. Repeat to make four A2/A3 units.

Figure 1

3. Sew B to each of the A2-A3 units to make an A2/A3-B unit as shown in Figure 2; press seams toward B.

Figure 2

4. Repeat steps 2 and 3 with A3, A1 and B pieces to complete four A1/A3-B units referring to Figure 3.

Figure 3

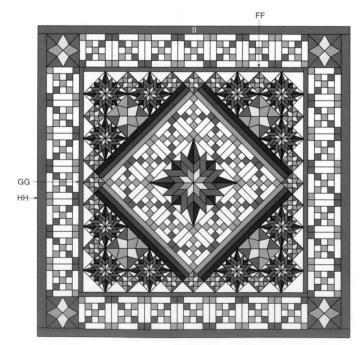

Galaxia
Placement Diagram 71½" x 71½"

5. Join one each A1/A3-B unit and A2/A3-B unit with a Y seam to complete a star point as shown in Figure 4, starting and stopping stitching at the marked dot; press seam open. Repeat to make four star points.

Figure 4

6. Join two star points using a Y seam, stitching to the dot, to make a half-star unit as shown in Figure 5; press seam open.

Figure 5

7. Join the two half-star units using a Y seam, stitching to the dots, to make the star unit as shown in Figure 6; press seam open.

Figure 6

8. Sew D to E to make a D-E unit as shown in Figure 7; press seam open. Repeat to make four units.

Figure 7   **Figure 8**

9. Sew F and FR (mirror-image) to opposite sides of one D-E unit to make a corner unit as shown in Figure 8; press seams toward F pieces. Repeat to make four corner units. ***Note:*** *The pieced unit should measure 4¹¹⁄₁₆" (just under 4¾").*

10. Sew a corner unit between two diamonds on the star unit, using a Y seam, starting stitching at the inside dots and stitching to the outside of the

pieces as shown in Figure 9; press seam toward the star unit. Repeat with remaining corner units as shown in Figure 10.

Figure 9

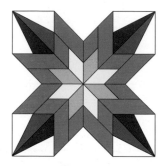

Figure 10

11. Sew a C2 triangle to a C3 triangle and press seam open as shown in Figure 11.

Figure 11   **Figure 12**

12. Sew a C1 triangle to two adjacent sides of the C2/C3 unit to complete a C unit as shown in Figure 12; press seams toward C1 triangles. Repeat to make four C units.

13. Sew a C unit into the remaining openings in the star unit using a Y seam to complete the Center Star block as shown in Figure 13; press seams away from the C units. Block should measure 14¾" at this time.

Figure 13

Completing the Outer Star Blocks

1. To complete one Outer Star block, select four each G1, G2, I2, I3, J, K, L and LR; and eight each G3, H and I1 pieces.

2. Repeat steps 2–13 of Complete the Center Star Block, substituting pieces referring to Figure 14, to complete a total of 12 Outer Star blocks. Each block should measure 7⅝" at this time.

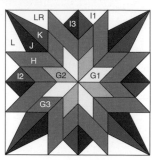

Figure 14

Completing the Center Nine-Patch Blocks

1. To complete one Center Nine-Patch block, select four each M2, M3 and N; and five M1 pieces.

2. Sew an M3 square between one each M1 and M2 square to complete the top row as shown in Figure 15; press seams toward M2. Repeat to make the bottom row.

Figure 15

3. Sew an M3 square to opposite sides of an M1 square to make the center row as shown in Figure 16; press seams toward M1.

Figure 16

4. Sew the center row between the top and bottom rows to complete the center unit as shown in Figure 17; press seams toward the center row.

Figure 17

5. Sew an N rectangle to opposite sides of the center unit as shown in Figure 18; press seams toward N.

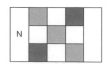

Figure 18

6. Sew an M1 square to one end and an M2 square to the opposite end of each remaining N rectangle as shown in Figure 19; press seams toward N.

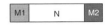
Figure 19

7. Sew the M-N strips to the remaining sides of the center unit to complete one Center Nine-Patch block as shown in Figure 20; press seams away from the center unit.

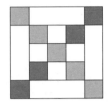
Figure 20

8. Repeat steps 1–7 to complete a total of 12 Center Nine-Patch blocks. Each block should measure 7⅝" at this point.

Completing the Border Nine-Patch Blocks

1. To complete one Border Nine-Patch block, select four each U2, U3 and V pieces; and five U1 pieces.

2. Repeat steps 2–7 for Completing the Center Nine-Patch Blocks, substituting pieces referring to Figure 21 to complete a total of 28 Border Nine-Patch blocks. Each block should measure 8" x 8" at this time.

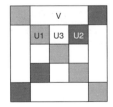
Figure 21

Completing the Small Gold Star Blocks

1. To complete one Small Gold Star block, select two each O1, O2, P1, P2, Q1 and Q2 pieces.

2. Sew an O1 piece to the left-side edge of Q2 as shown in Figure 22; press seams toward O1. Sew a P1 piece to the right-side edge of the pieced unit to complete one Q2 unit, again referring to Figure 22. Repeat to make a second unit.

    Figure 22   **Figure 23**

3. Repeat step 2 with O2, P2 and Q1 to complete two Q1 units referring to Figure 23.

4. Sew a Q1 unit to a Q2 unit to make a block half as shown in Figure 24; press seams toward the Q2 unit. Repeat to make a second block half.

Figure 24

5. Join the two block halves to complete one Small Gold Star block referring to Figure 25; press seam to one side. Blocks should measure 4¹⁄₁₆" at this time.

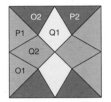
Figure 25

6. Repeat steps 1–5 to complete a total of 20 Small Gold Star blocks.

Completing the Large Gold Star Blocks

1. To complete one Large Gold Star block, select two each R1, R2, S1, S2, T1 and T2 pieces.

2. Repeat steps 2–5 for Completing the Small Gold Star blocks, substituting pieces referring to Figure 26 to complete a total of four Large Gold Star blocks. Each block should measure 7⅝" x 7⅝" at this time.

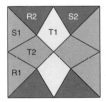
Figure 26

Completing the Corner Star Blocks

1. To complete one Corner Star block, select two each Y1 and Y2, and four each W and X pieces.

2. Repeat steps 2–5 for Completing the Small Gold Star blocks, sewing W pieces to the left and X pieces to the right edges of the Y1 and Y2 pieces and referring to Figure 27 to complete a total of four Corner Star blocks. Each block should measure 8" x 8" at this time.

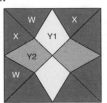
Figure 27

House of White Birches, Berne, Indiana 46711   Clotilde.com

Completing the Quilt Center

1. Join two Center Nine-Patch blocks to make a short block unit as shown in Figure 28; press seam to one side. Repeat with a second set of blocks to make a second short block unit.

Figure 28

2. Sew a short block unit to opposite sides of the Center Star block as shown in Figure 29; press seams toward the short block units.

Figure 29

3. Join four Center Nine-Patch blocks to make a long block unit referring to Figure 30; press seams to one side. Repeat to make a second long block unit.

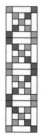

Figure 30

4. Sew a long block unit to opposite sides of the pieced unit as shown in Figure 31; press seams toward the long block units.

Figure 31

5. Join an AA, BB and CC strips along length to make a pieced border strip; press seams to one side. Repeat to make four pieced border strips.

6. Sew a pieced border strip to opposite sides of the center unit with the AA strips toward the center unit; press seams toward strips.

7. Sew a Small Gold Star block to each end of each remaining pieced strip as shown in Figure 32; press seams toward the strips.

Figure 32

8. Sew these strips to the center unit to complete the center unit; press seams toward strips.

Completing the Pieced Corner Unit

1. Sew a DD triangle to one O1/P1 and one O2/P2 side of a Small Gold Star block to make a left triangle unit as shown in Figure 33; press seams toward DD. Repeat to make eight left triangle units.

Figure 33

2. Repeat step 1 to make eight right triangle units referring to Figure 34.

Figure 34

3. Sew a left triangle unit to a side of an Outer Star block and a right triangle unit to the opposite side of the block as shown in Figure 35; press seams toward the triangle units.

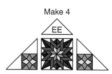

Figure 35

4. Sew an EE triangle to the top edge of the Outer Star block to complete a corner unit, again referring to Figure 35.

5. Repeat steps 3 and 4 to make a total of four corner units.

6. Sew a Large Gold Star block between two Outer Star blocks and add a left triangle unit to one end and a right triangle unit to the opposite end to complete a corner row as shown in Figure 36; press seams toward the Large Gold Star block and the triangle units. Repeat to make four corner rows.

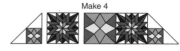

Make 4

Figure 36

7. Sew a corner row to a corner unit to complete a large corner unit as shown in Figure 37; press seam toward the corner row. Repeat to make a total of four large corner units.

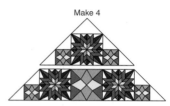

Make 4

Figure 37

8. Sew a large corner unit to each side of the center unit to complete the quilt center as shown in Figure 38; press seams toward the center unit.

Figure 38

Completing the Quilt Top

1. Sew an FF strip to the top and bottom and a GG strip to opposite sides of the center unit; press seams toward strips.

2. Join seven Border Nine-Patch blocks to make an X border row as shown in Figure 39; press seams to one side. Repeat to make a second X border row.

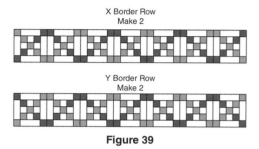

X Border Row
Make 2

Y Border Row
Make 2

Figure 39

3. Repeat step 2 to make two Y border rows, again referring to Figure 39.

4. Sew a Y border row to opposite sides of the pieced center unit referring to the Placement Diagram for positioning; press seams toward the GG strips.

5. Sew a Corner Star block to each end of each X border row; press seams toward the border rows.

6. Sew the block/border rows to the top and bottom of the pieced center unit; press seams toward FF strips.

7. Sew an HH strip to opposite long sides and an II strip to the top and bottom of the pieced section to complete the quilt top; press seams toward strips.

8. Your quilt top is now finished and ready to be quilted. See page 47 for finishing instructions. ❖

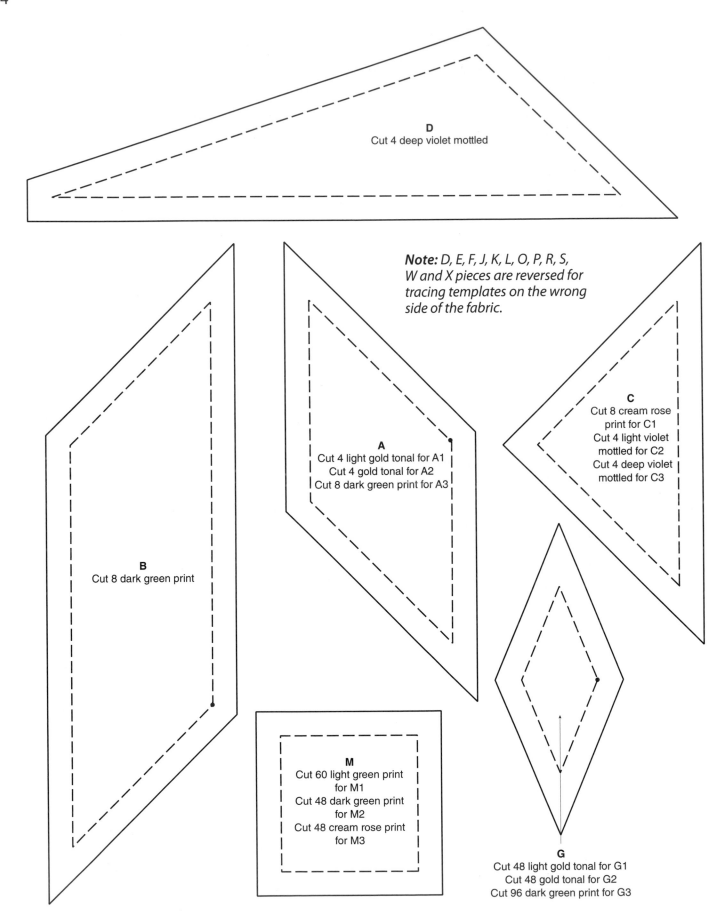

D
Cut 4 deep violet mottled

Note: D, E, F, J, K, L, O, P, R, S, W and X pieces are reversed for tracing templates on the wrong side of the fabric.

C
Cut 8 cream rose print for C1
Cut 4 light violet mottled for C2
Cut 4 deep violet mottled for C3

A
Cut 4 light gold tonal for A1
Cut 4 gold tonal for A2
Cut 8 dark green print for A3

B
Cut 8 dark green print

M
Cut 60 light green print for M1
Cut 48 dark green print for M2
Cut 48 cream rose print for M3

G
Cut 48 light gold tonal for G1
Cut 48 gold tonal for G2
Cut 96 dark green print for G3

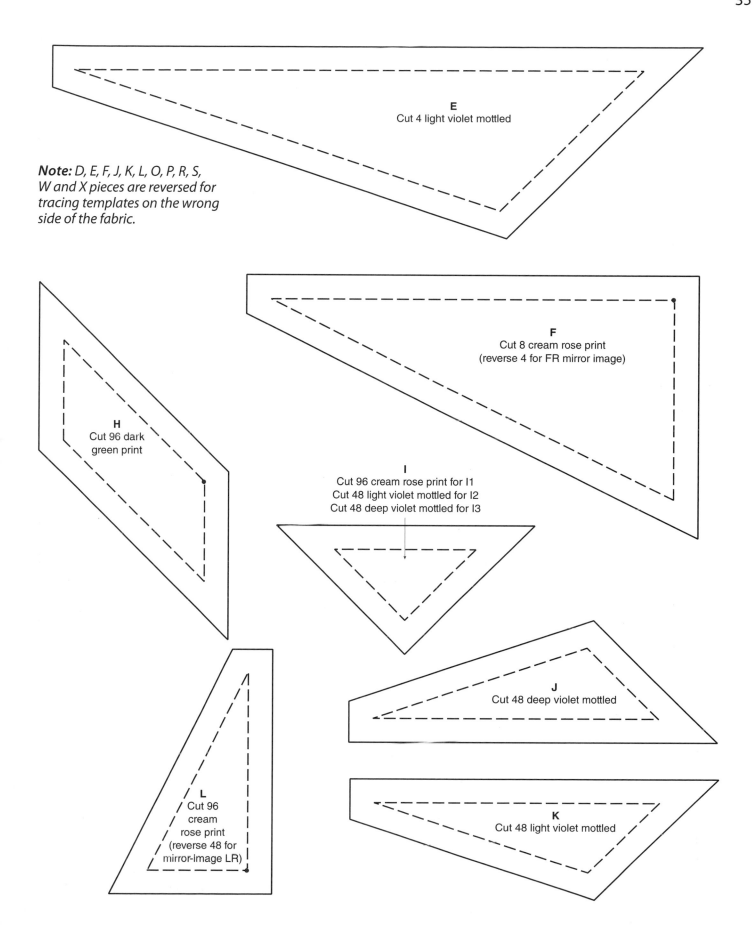

E
Cut 4 light violet mottled

Note: *D, E, F, J, K, L, O, P, R, S, W and X pieces are reversed for tracing templates on the wrong side of the fabric.*

F
Cut 8 cream rose print
(reverse 4 for FR mirror image)

H
Cut 96 dark
green print

I
Cut 96 cream rose print for I1
Cut 48 light violet mottled for I2
Cut 48 deep violet mottled for I3

J
Cut 48 deep violet mottled

L
Cut 96
cream
rose print
(reverse 48 for
mirror-image LR)

K
Cut 48 light violet mottled

36

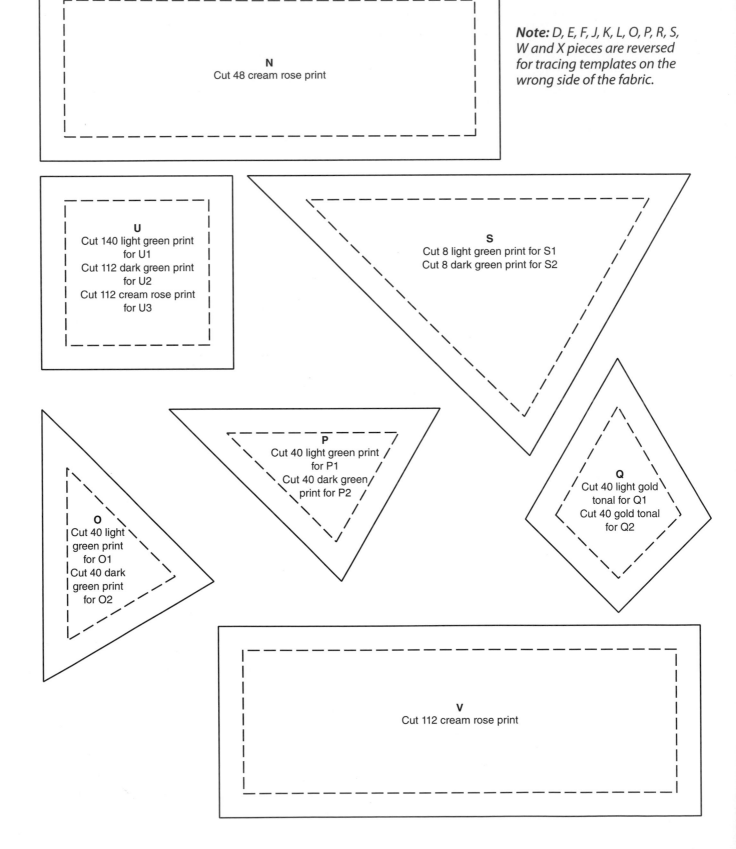

N
Cut 48 cream rose print

Note: D, E, F, J, K, L, O, P, R, S, W and X pieces are reversed for tracing templates on the wrong side of the fabric.

U
Cut 140 light green print for U1
Cut 112 dark green print for U2
Cut 112 cream rose print for U3

S
Cut 8 light green print for S1
Cut 8 dark green print for S2

P
Cut 40 light green print for P1
Cut 40 dark green print for P2

O
Cut 40 light green print for O1
Cut 40 dark green print for O2

Q
Cut 40 light gold tonal for Q1
Cut 40 gold tonal for Q2

V
Cut 112 cream rose print

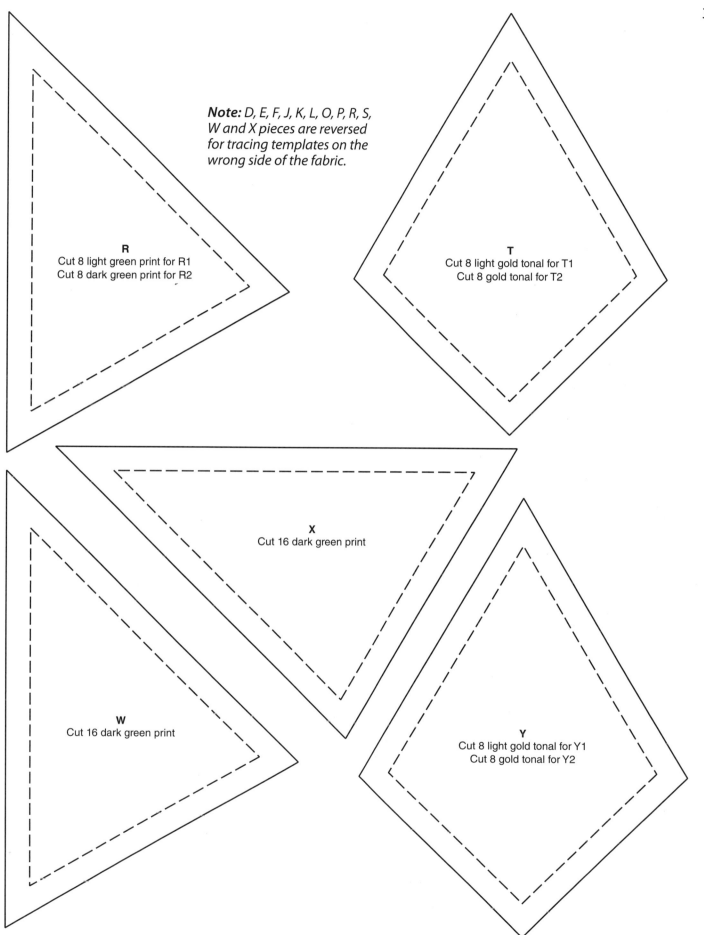

Note: *D, E, F, J, K, L, O, P, R, S, W and X pieces are reversed for tracing templates on the wrong side of the fabric.*

R
Cut 8 light green print for R1
Cut 8 dark green print for R2

T
Cut 8 light gold tonal for T1
Cut 8 gold tonal for T2

X
Cut 16 dark green print

W
Cut 16 dark green print

Y
Cut 8 light gold tonal for Y1
Cut 8 gold tonal for Y2

Star Flower

Project Note

Refer to instructions for making Y seams on page 47 wherever Y seams are referenced in these instructions.

Project Specifications

Skill Level: Advanced
Quilt Size: 65" x 65"
Block Size: 10" x 10"
Number of Blocks: 25

Materials

- ⅜ yard light lavender mottled
- ⅜ yard deep lavender mottled
- ¾ yard light green mottled
- 1 yard dark green mottled
- 1⅛ yards gray mottled
- 1¼ yards cream tonal
- 2½ yards black solid
- Batting 73" x 73"
- Backing 73" x 73"
- All-purpose thread to match fabrics
- Quilting thread
- Template material
- Water-soluble blue pen
- Basic sewing tools and supplies

Cutting

1. Prepare templates using patterns given; cut as directed on each piece. Transfer seam dots (shown as red dots on patterns) to fabrics.

2. Cut six 4¾" by fabric width strips black solid; join strips on short ends to make one long strip; press seams open. Subcut strip into two 57" N strips and two 65½" O strips.

3. Cut seven 2¼" by fabric width strips black solid for binding.

Completing the Star Flower Blocks

1. For one block, select four each light lavender A1, deep lavender A2, cream C2 and cream D; eight each dark green B1 and cream B2; and 12 black C1 pieces.

2. To complete one Star Flower block, sew A1 to A2 using a Y seam, stopping stitching at the marked dots; press seam open. Trim off excess seam allowance even with the edges of the stitched unit as

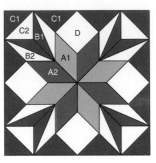
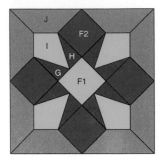

Star Flower
10" x 10" Block
Make 12

Star Leaf
10" x 10" Block
Make 13

shown in Figure 1. Repeat with remaining A1 and A2 pieces to make four A units.

Figure 1

3. Join two A units, stopping stitching at marked dots as shown in Figure 2; press seams open. Repeat.

Figure 2

4. Join the stitched units to complete the star unit as shown in Figure 3; press seams open.

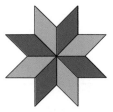

Figure 3

5. Sew B1 to B2 as shown in Figure 4; press seams open. Repeat to make eight pieced units.

Figure 4

6. Join two pieced units, stopping stitching at Y seams, to make a B unit as shown in Figure 5; press seams open. Repeat to make four B units.

Figure 5

7. Sew a cream C2 triangle to a black C1 triangle to make a C unit as shown in Figure 6; press seam toward C2. Repeat to make four C units.

Figure 6

8. Set a C unit into a B unit using a Y seam, starting stitching on one side of the inside angle of the B unit as shown in Figure 7. Repeat stitching the second seam from the inside to the outside edge to complete a B-C unit. Press seams toward the B unit. Repeat to make four B-C units.

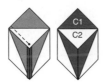

Figure 7

9. Set a B-C unit into every other star point of the star unit using a Y seam as in step 8 and referring to Figure 8; press seams toward the star unit.

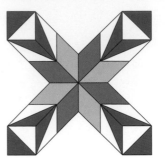

Figure 8

10. Sew a C1 triangle to two adjacent sides of a cream D square to make a C-D unit as shown in Figure 9; press seams toward C1 triangles. Repeat to make four C-D units units.

Figure 9

11. Set a C-D unit into each remaining opening in the star unit using a Y seam as in step 8 and referring to Figure 10 to complete one Star Flower block.

Figure 10

12. Repeat steps 1–11 to complete a total of 12 Star Flower blocks.

Completing the Star Flower Side Units

1. For one side unit, select 1 cream C2; two each light lavender A1, deep lavender A2, black E1, cream E2, cream D; four each dark green B1 and cream B2; and five black C1 pieces.

2. To complete one Star Flower side unit, sew A1 to A2 using a Y seam to make one A unit, stopping stitching at the marked dots; press seam open. Trim off excess seam allowance even with the edges of the stitched unit, again referring to Figure 1. Repeat to make two A units.

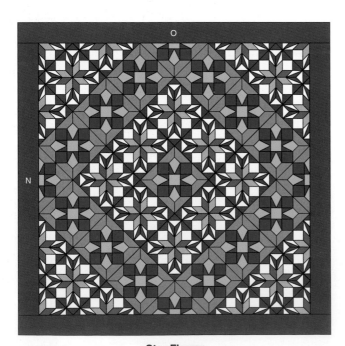

Star Flower
Placement Diagram 65" x 65"

House of White Birches, Berne, Indiana 46711 Clotilde.com

3. Join the two A units, stopping stitching at marked dots, again referring to Figure 2 to make a half-star unit; press seams open.

4. Sew B1 to B2, again referring to Figure 4; press seams open.

5. Join two pieced units to make a B unit, again referring to Figure 5; press seams open.

6. Sew a cream C2 triangle to a black C1 triangle to make a C unit, again referring to Figure 6; press seam toward C2.

7. Set the C unit into the B unit using a Y seam, starting stitching on one side of the inside angle of the B unit, again referring to Figure 7. Repeat stitching the second seam from the inside to the outside edge to complete a B-C unit. Press seams toward the B unit.

8. Set a B-C unit into the star point of the star unit using a Y seam as in step 7, referring to Figure 11; press seams toward the star unit.

Figure 11

9. Sew a black E1 to a cream E2 to make an E unit as shown in Figure 12; press seam toward E1. Repeat to make a reverse E unit, again referring to Figure 12.

E Unit

Reverse E Unit

Figure 12

10. Sew an E unit to the B1 side of one B unit and the reverse E unit to the B1 side of the second B unit to make B-E and reversed B-E units as shown in Figure 13; press seams toward the B units.

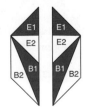

Figure 13

11. Sew the B-E and reversed B-E units to the previously stitched half-star unit as shown in Figure 14; press seams toward the half-star unit.

Figure 14

12. Sew a C1 triangle to two adjacent sides of a cream D square to make a C-D unit, again referring to Figure 9; press seams toward C1 triangles. Repeat to make a second C-D unit.

13. Set a C-D unit into both remaining openings in the half-star unit using a Y seam referring to Figure 15 to complete one Star Flower side unit; press seams toward the half-star unit.

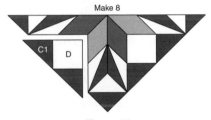

Make 8

Figure 15

14. Repeat steps 1–13 to complete a total of eight Star Flower side units.

Completing the Small Corner Units

1. For one small corner unit, select one each light lavender A1, deep lavender A2 and cream D; two each dark green B1, cream B2, black C1, black E1 and cream E2 pieces.

2. To complete one small corner unit, sew A1 to A2 using a Y seam to make an A unit, stopping stitching at the marked dots; press seam open. Trim off excess seam allowance even with the edges of the stitched unit, again referring to Figure 1.

3. Sew B1 to B2 to make a B unit, again referring to Figure 4; press seams open. Repeat to make two B units.

4. Sew a black E1 to a cream E2 to make an E unit, again referring to Figure 12; press seam toward E1. Repeat to make a reverse E unit.

5. Sew an E unit to the B1 side of one B unit and the reverse E unit to the B1 side of the second B unit to make B-E and reversed B-E unit, again referring to Figure 13; press seams toward the B units.

6. Sew the B-E and reversed B-E units to the A unit as shown in Figure 16; press seams toward the A unit.

Figure 16

7. Sew a C1 triangle to two adjacent sides of the cream D square to make a C-D unit, again referring to Figure 9; press seams toward C1 triangles.

8. Set a C-D unit into the opening in the pieced unit using a Y seam and referring to Figure 17 to complete one small corner unit; press seams away from the C-D unit.

Make 4

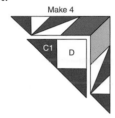

Figure 17

9. Repeat steps 1–8 to complete a total of four small corner units.

Completing the Star Leaf Blocks

1. For one block, select one light green F1; four each dark green F2, black G, black H and light green I; and eight gray J pieces.

2. To complete one Star Leaf block, sew G and H to I to make an I unit as shown in Figure 18; press seams toward G and H. Repeat to make four I units.

Figure 18   **Figure 19**

3. Sew an I unit to opposite sides of the F1 square to make the center row as shown in Figure 19; press seams toward F1.

4. Sew an F2 square to opposite sides of an I unit to make an F-I unit as shown in Figure 20; press seams toward F2. Repeat to make a second F-I unit.

Figure 20

5. Sew an F-I unit to opposite sides of the center row as shown in Figure 21; press seams toward the F-I units.

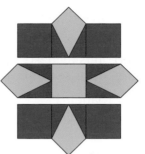

Figure 21

6. Sew a J piece onto one side of each F2 square using a Y seam, stitching from the inside angle of one seam to the outside point; repeat stitching on the I side of the seam. Press seams away from J. Repeat on one side of each of the remaining three F2 squares as shown in Figure 22.

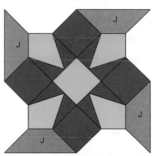

Figure 22

7. Add the remaining J pieces to the second side of F2 and I pieces using a Y seam and press to complete one Star Leaf block referring to Figure 23; press seams away from J.

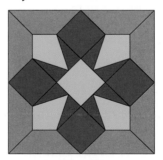

Figure 23

8. Repeat steps 1–7 to complete a total of 13 Star Leaf blocks.

44

Completing the Star Leaf Side Units

1. For one side unit, select one each light green I, K, L and M; two each black G, black H and dark green F2; and four gray J pieces.

2. To complete one Star Leaf side unit, sew L to G and M to H to make one each L-G and M-H unit as shown in Figure 24; press seams toward L and M.

Figure 24

3. Sew the L-G and M-H units to opposite sides of K to make a K unit as shown in Figure 25; press seams toward K.

Figure 25

4. Sew G and H to I to make an I unit, again referring to Figure 18; press seams toward G and H.

5. Sew an F2 square to opposite sides of an I unit to make an F-I unit, again referring to Figure 20; press seams toward F2.

6. Sew the K unit to the G/H side of the F-I unit as shown in Figure 26; press seams toward the K unit.

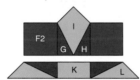

Figure 26

7. Add the J pieces to the pieced unit referring to steps 6 and 7 for Completing the Star Leaf Blocks to complete a Star Leaf side unit as shown in Figure 27.

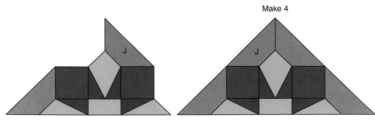

Make 4

Figure 27

8. Repeat steps 1–7 to complete a total of four side Star Leaf side units.

Completing the Quilt Top

1. Join three Star Flower blocks to make an X row as shown in Figure 28; press seams to one side. Repeat to make two X rows.

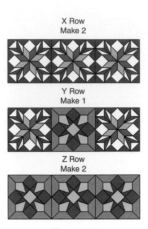

X Row
Make 2

Y Row
Make 1

Z Row
Make 2

Figure 28

2. Join one Star Leaf block and two Star Flower blocks to make a Y row, again referring to Figure 28; press seams to one side.

3. Join three Star Leaf blocks to make a Z row, again referring to Figure 28; press seams to one side.

4. Join the X, Y and Z rows referring to Figure 29, turning rows so seams in adjoining rows face in opposite directions as shown in Figure 30; press seams in one direction.

Figure 29

Figure 30

5. Join three Star Leaf blocks with two Star Leaf side units to make a side row as shown in Figure 31; press seams to one side. Repeat to make a second side row.

Make 2

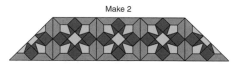

Figure 31

6. Sew a side row to opposite sides of the previously pieced section referring to Figure 32; press seams toward the side rows.

7. Sew a Star Flower side unit to opposite sides of a Star Flower block and add a small corner unit to complete a large corner unit as shown in Figure 33; press seams to one side. Repeat to make a total of four large corner units.

Make 4

Figure 33

8. Sew a large corner unit to each side of the previously pieced section to complete the quilt center referring to the Placement Diagram; press seams away from the large corner units.

9. Sew N strips to opposite sides and O strips to the top and bottom of the pieced center to complete the quilt top; press seams toward N and O strips.

10. The quilt top is ready for quilting and binding as desired. See page 47 for finishing instructions. ❖

Figure 32

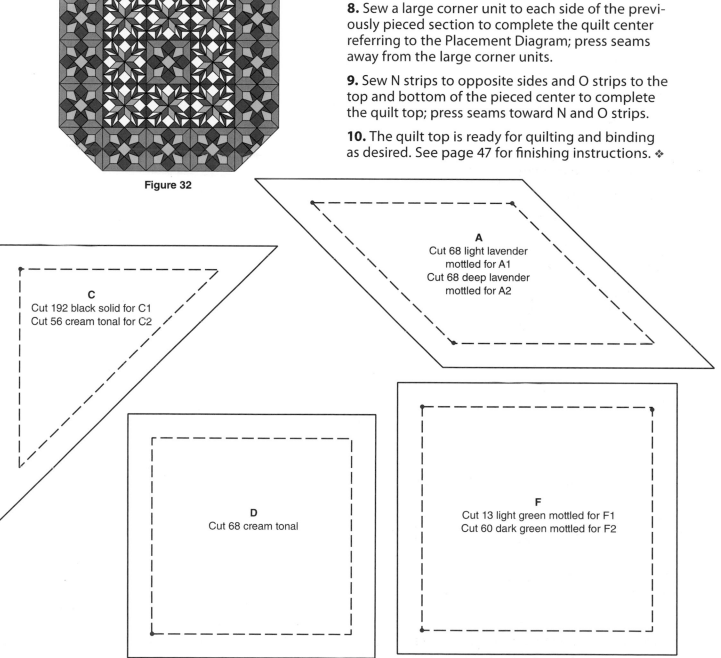

C
Cut 192 black solid for C1
Cut 56 cream tonal for C2

A
Cut 68 light lavender mottled for A1
Cut 68 deep lavender mottled for A2

D
Cut 68 cream tonal

F
Cut 13 light green mottled for F1
Cut 60 dark green mottled for F2

House of White Birches, Berne, Indiana 46711   Clotilde.com

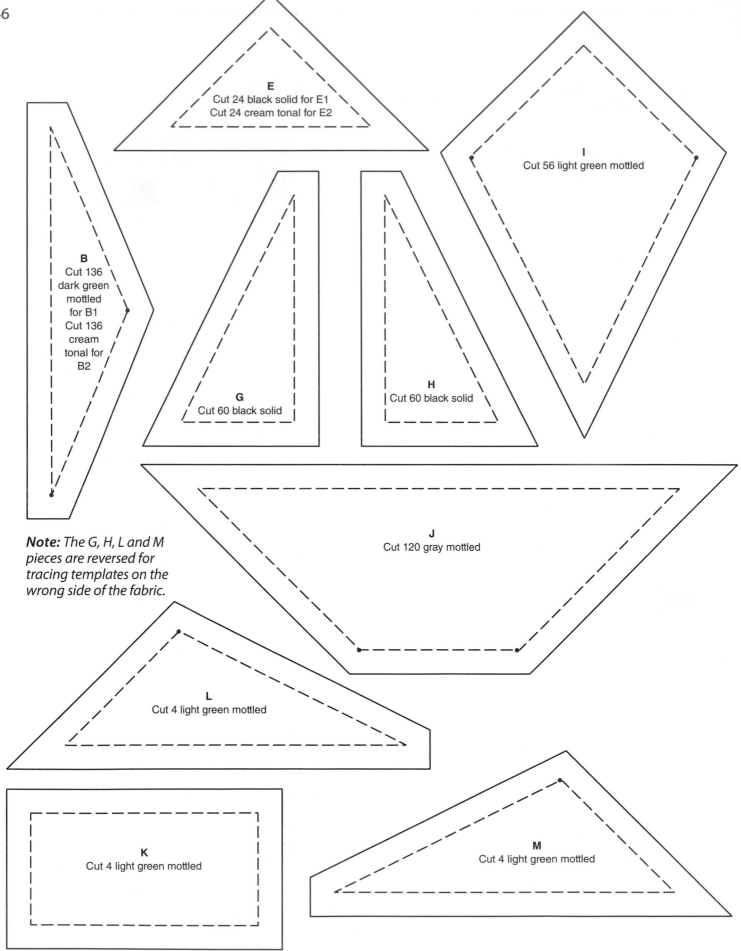

E
Cut 24 black solid for E1
Cut 24 cream tonal for E2

I
Cut 56 light green mottled

B
Cut 136 dark green mottled for B1
Cut 136 cream tonal for B2

G
Cut 60 black solid

H
Cut 60 black solid

J
Cut 120 gray mottled

Note: The G, H, L and M pieces are reversed for tracing templates on the wrong side of the fabric.

L
Cut 4 light green mottled

K
Cut 4 light green mottled

M
Cut 4 light green mottled

Stitching a Y Seam

Many star designs require set-in pieces. This is accomplished with a Y seam—the three seams together make a Y shape (Figure 1). This type of seam is accomplished in three easy steps. Stopping stitching at the seam intersections, pressing and stitching from the inside point to the outside point are all equally important to a perfect Y seam.

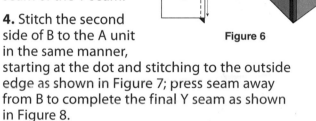

Figure 1

Refer to the following instructions to make star quilts with perfect set-in pieces.

Constructing a Perfect Y Seam

1. Using a large needle or small paper punch, make a hole in the templates at the seam intersections marked with red dots on patterns as shown in Figure 2.

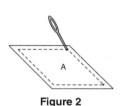

Figure 2   **Figure 3**   **Figure 4**

2. For the example shown, select two A pieces and join, starting stitching at the dot and ending at the end of the seam as shown in Figure 3 and backstitching at the beginning of the seam to lock the stitches; press this seam open referring to Figure 4.

This is the first step in the Y seam. Trim seam ends even with A pieces, again referring to Figure 4.

3. Set in a B piece, starting stitching at the marked dots on the joined A unit and backstitching to lock seams as shown in Figure 5. Stitch to the end of the seam as usual as shown in Figure 6. Press seams away from B, again referring to Figure 6. This is the second seam of the Y seam.

Figure 5

4. Stitch the second side of B to the A unit in the same manner, starting at the dot and stitching to the outside edge as shown in Figure 7; press seam away from B to complete the final Y seam as shown in Figure 8.

Figure 6

Figure 7   **Figure 8**

Finishing Your Quilt

Step 1. Sandwich the batting between the completed top and prepared backing; pin or baste layers together to hold. *Note: If using basting spray to hold layers together, refer to instructions on the product container for use.*

Step 2. Quilt as desired by hand or machine; remove pins or basting. Trim excess backing and batting even with quilt top.

Step 3. Join binding strips on short ends to make one long strip. Fold the strip in half along length with wrong sides together; press.

Step 4. Sew binding to quilt edges, mitering corners and overlapping ends. Fold binding to the back side and stitch in place to finish.

House of White Birches, Berne, Indiana 46711   Clotilde.com

Photo Index

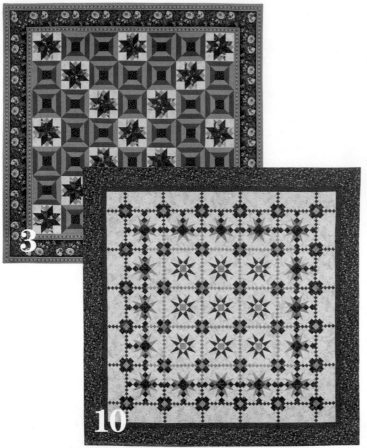

3

10

18

26

38

HOUSE of WHITE BIRCHES
PUBLISHERS
SINCE 1947

Stars Unlimited is published by DRG, 306 East Parr Road, Berne, IN 46711. Printed in USA. Copyright © 2011 DRG. All rights reserved. This publication may not be reproduced in part or in whole without written permission from the publisher.

RETAIL STORES: If you would like to carry this pattern book or any other DRG publications, visit DRGwholesale.com

Every effort has been made to ensure that the instructions in this pattern book are complete and accurate. We cannot, however, take responsibility for human error, typographical mistakes or variations in individual work. Please visit ClotildeCustomerCare.com to check for pattern updates.

ISBN: 978-1-59217-325-9

1 2 3 4 5 6 7 8 9